Our Company

PETER PAUPER PRESS
Fine Books and Gifts Since 1928

In 1928, at the age of twenty-two, Peter Beilenson began printing books on a small press in the basement of his parents' home in Larchmont, New York. Peter—and later, his wife, Edna—sought to create fine books that sold at "prices even a pauper could afford."

Today, still family owned and operated, Peter Pauper Press continues to honor our founders' legacy of quality, value, and fun for big kids and small kids alike.

Originally published in France as *Au temps des dinosaures*,
French edition ISBN 978-2-215-423 © Fleurus Editions, Paris–2015

Library of Congress Cataloging-in-Publication Data

Names: Amiot, Romain. | Mehee, Loic, 1979- illustrator.
Title: Dinosaurs / Romain Amiot ; [illustrated by] Loic Mehee.
Other titles: Au temps des dinosaures. English
Description: White Plains, New York : Peter Pauper Press, Inc., [2017]

Series: Seek and find | Translation of: Au temps des dinosaures /Romain
Amiot ; illustrations de Loic Mehee (Paris : Fleurus, 2015).
Audience:
Age 5+ | Audience: K to grade 3.
Identifiers: LCCN 2017001673 | ISBN 9781441324740 (hardcover : alk. paper)
Subjects: LCSH: Paleontology--Juvenile literature. |
Paleontology--Mesozoic--Juvenile literature. | Dinosaurs--Juvenile literature.
Classification: LCC QE714.5 .A4518 2017 | DDC 567.9--dc23 LC record
available at https://lccn.loc.gov/2017001673

English translation by Vesna Neskow.

Published in the United Kingdom and Europe by
Peter Pauper Press, Inc. c/o White Pebble International
Unit 2, Plot 11 Terminus Road
Chichester, West Sussex PO19 8TX, UK

ROMAIN AMIOT

SEEK and FIND

LOÏC MÉHÉE

DINOSAURS

PETER PAUPER PRESS, INC.
White Plains, New York

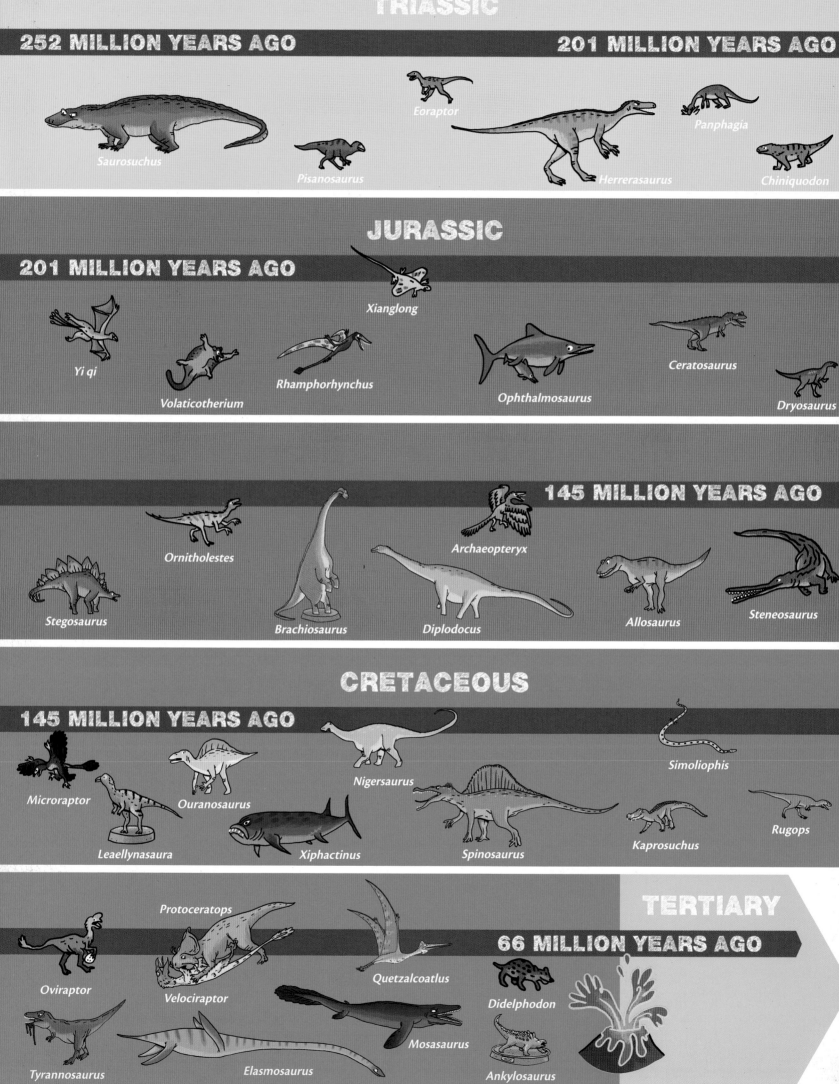

TRIASSIC

252 MILLION YEARS AGO   **201 MILLION YEARS AGO**

Eoraptor

Saurosuchus

Pisanosaurus

Panphagia

Herrerasaurus

Chiniquodon

JURASSIC

201 MILLION YEARS AGO

Xianglong

Yi qi

Volaticotherium

Rhamphorhynchus

Ophthalmosaurus

Ceratosaurus

Dryosaurus

145 MILLION YEARS AGO

Ornitholestes

Archaeopteryx

Stegosaurus

Brachiosaurus

Diplodocus

Allosaurus

Steneosaurus

CRETACEOUS

145 MILLION YEARS AGO

Nigersaurus

Simoliophis

Microraptor

Ouranosaurus

Leaellynasaura

Xiphactinus

Spinosaurus

Kaprosuchus

Rugops

TERTIARY

Protoceratops

66 MILLION YEARS AGO

Oviraptor

Velociraptor

Quetzalcoatlus

Didelphodon

Tyrannosaurus

Elasmosaurus

Mosasaurus

Ankylosaurus

No extinct creatures are more popular today than dinosaurs. Ferocious and fascinating, they enthrall young and old, but their history remains a puzzle of evolution.

Who were dinosaurs, these animals halfway between reptiles and birds?

What were their origins and how did they come to rule the world?

What other extraordinary creatures shared the planet with the "terrible lizards"?

Why did they go extinct, after more than 160 million years as masters of the Earth?

Thanks to paleontologists, scientists who study the history of life on our planet, we learn more about dinosaurs every year. Paleontologists dig up and examine fossils, traces of prehistoric creatures preserved in rock. The fossils of many new dinosaur species still lie buried beneath the earth, waiting for one thing: to be discovered!

WHAT A STORY!

Hidden in this book you will find plants and animals that lived in the Mesozoic Era, the time of the dinosaurs' reign. Fiery volcanoes, ancient fossils, paleontologists digging in the earth: It's up to you to unearth them all!

WHAT ARE DINOSAURS?

Dinosaurs first appeared about 235 million years ago. Halfway between reptiles and birds, some ancient dinosaurs were the size of a pigeon, while others grew as large as a small building. It's no wonder they ruled every continent during the Mesozoic Era. Scientists have discovered more than a thousand dinosaur species so far. But the "terrible lizards" still hide many secrets . . .

ON SOLID GROUND

Dinosaurs roamed the land, except for a few species that were more at home in lakes and rivers. Paleontologists have found numerous dinosaur **footprints** in rock, and sometimes even long tracks of prints, proving that dinosaurs traveled by walking on land.

STANDING UP STRAIGHT

Unlike reptiles such as crocodiles and lizards, which move by crawling on the ground, dinosaurs' legs stood straight up beneath their bodies like the legs of birds or mammals. Some dinosaurs, like the gigantic sauropod *Brachiosaurus*, moved around on all fours. Others used only their hind legs. (To learn more about sauropods, see page 9.)

FIND THEM ALL!

FEATHERS OR SCALES

Scientists once believed that all dinosaurs' bodies were covered in scales. Recent discoveries show that while some large dinosaurs, such as **Ankylosaurus**, had scales, the bodies of many others, such as **Oviraptor**, were covered in feathers or long strands called proto-feathers.

WARM-BLOODED ANIMALS

Like birds or mammals today, dinosaurs were warm-blooded. In other words, they had a high, stable body temperature and could live in cold places. This helped them survive on all continents, even around the North and South Poles. **Leaellynasaura** was an Antarctic dinosaur. Cold-blooded reptiles can't live in frozen climates.

DINOSAUR MENUS

Each dinosaur had its own menu. Some were herbivores (eating plants), others carnivores (eating other animals), and still others mixed plants with fresh meat. Depending on what they ate, some dinosaurs, like **Gigantoraptor**, had beaks. Others, like **T-rex**, had jaws full of teeth. Better yet, dinos like hadrosaurs and ceratopsians had both beaks and teeth!

EGGS AND NESTS

Dinosaurs laid **eggs**. Some laid a *lot* of eggs! In a few places, paleontologists have found thousands of fossilized dinosaur eggs. Dinosaurs dug nests for their eggs in dirt or sand, and sometimes covered them with leaves and branches. Scientists think that some dinosaurs were very caring parents.

THE FIRST DINOSAURS

The earliest dinosaurs emerged during the Triassic period. Millions of years before they ruled the world, the first dinosaurs were rare and usually small. It was hard to survive among the hordes of huge two-tusked dicynodonts, dangerous amphibian temnospondyls hidden by the flow of water, and monstrous rauisuchians, the super-villains of the time. Luckily, dinosaurs had the ultimate advantage: their speed allowed them to escape from predators, who were much slower.

EORAPTOR

This 40-inch-long dinosaur was one of the first theropods, a group of dinosaurs that walked on two legs and tended to eat meat. (Animals that walk on two legs are called bipeds.) *Eoraptor* had the teeth of an herbivore in its lower jaw and the teeth of a carnivore in its upper jaw. This allowed it to eat both fresh meat and tender plants, which it found in immense forests of conifers, horsetail grasses, and ferns.

PANPHAGIA

A biped like other dinosaurs of its time, *Panphagia* grew about six and a half feet long. It had a lengthy neck and, based on its teeth, ate a bit of everything. It's hard to imagine that this tiny sauropodomorph could be the ancestor of *Diplodocus* and *Brachiosaurus*, the giant herbivores of the Jurassic!

PISANOSAURUS

This little biped dinosaur is an ornithischian, an ancestor of *Triceratops*, *Iguanodon*, or *Stegosaurus*. At about three and a half feet long, *Pisanosaurus* ate ground vegetation and survived by being light, agile, and fast. This advantage helped it escape most of its slower and more massive predators, leaving them in the dust.

THE MONSTROUS RAUISUCHIANS

If crocodiles seem scary, their likely ancestors, the **rauisuchians**, were much more terrifying! About 13 to 19 feet long, they moved easily on land, with their four legs upright beneath their bodies. Their enormous jaws full of sharp teeth helped them grab and devour their prey. They are considered the super-predators of the Triassic!

HERRERASAURUS

Herrerasaurus was the biggest carnivorous dinosaur of its time. It measured over nine feet long and weighed more than 660 pounds! A biped with hands that ended in sharp talons and jaws full of dagger-like teeth, it took advantage of its agility to hunt smaller dinosaurs, as well as many reptiles. (Though not rauisuchians!)

THE ANCESTORS OF MAMMALS

Among the abundant reptiles of the Triassic period, many were "mammal-like reptiles," such as **Chiniquodon**. Some were herbivores, others carnivores; but they are all ancestors of mammals, a group of animals that includes human beings. At the end of the Triassic, dinosaurs began to replace them as the dominant land animals. Though the dinosaurs ruled the rest of the Mesozoic Era, mammals took over when many dinosaurs went extinct, and still reign today.

LIFE IN THE JURASSIC PERIOD
(201 TO 145 MILLION YEARS AGO)

During this period, dinosaurs became huge. More and more dinosaur species existed, and they lived on every continent. (For much of the Jurassic, all the continents were smushed together into the supercontinent Pangaea.) The hot, humid weather of the time even allowed dinosaurs to live near the North and South Poles. In the Jurassic, the famous *Stegosaurus*, *Allosaurus*, and *Diplodocus* roamed the land; feathered dinosaurs made their appearance; and the first birds took flight.

ALLOSAURUS, THE JURASSIC BITER

With a 30-foot-long body, sharp claws, and a mouth full of 70 razor-sharp teeth, **Allosaurus** was the king of the Jurassic! Alone or in small groups, it hunted enormous sauropods, biting them deeply and waiting for them to die of exhaustion. This ferocious theropod required a big feast!

GIANT SAUROPODS

Sauropods, hands-down the biggest land animals that ever lived, were herbivorous quadrupeds with long necks and tails. (A quadruped is an animal that walks on four legs.) Its long neck allowed *Brachiosaurus* to eat the young, tender shoots at the tops of trees, where other dinosaurs could not reach them. As for **Diplodocus**, some think it cracked its tail like a whip to scare off its enemies.

STEGOSAURS

Two rows of large, bony diamond-shaped plates ran along the backs and tails of these massive herbivores. The plates may have featured bright colors to impress other **stegosaurs** or potential predators. If this didn't do the trick, they could defend themselves with the long, lethal bone spikes at the ends of their tails.

THE ORNITHOPOD DRYOSAURUS

Sauropods and stegosaurs were not the Jurassic's only herbivorous dinosaurs. Ornithopods, such as **Dryosaurus**, were much smaller bipeds and were even more numerous. They relied on their speed and agility to evade predators. It's no surprise that they became so abundant in the Cretaceous, with its slower-moving iguanodons and duck-billed dinosaurs. (To learn more about the Cretaceous, see page 15.)

OTHER PREDATORS

Other theropods, smaller than *Allosaurus*, hunted littler prey like ornithopods or young sauropods. **Ceratosaurus** is one of these. Recognizable by the bony horn on its nose, it is the ancestor of the Cretaceous period's ferocious abelisaurids (see page 15)!

ARCHAEOPTERYX

This minuscule dinosaur covered in feathers may have been the first bird. With its long tail, jaws full of teeth, and feather-covered winglike front limbs, it appears halfway between a reptile and a bird. Its small, clawed arms allowed it to climb trees, and from there take flight into the skies among pterosaurs (see page 12).

FIND TEHM
ALL!

CONQUEST OF THE SKIES

Unlike insects, who mastered flying 400 million years ago, reptiles launched into the air for the first time 210 million years ago. First it was the pterosaurs, followed by dinosaur ancestors of birds, and finally by mammals and lizards. Though they all have wings for flying, the wings differ from animal to animal. Some wings are covered in feathers, while others are made of thin skin stretched out between front and back legs.

LONG-TAILED PTEROSAURS

Rhamphorhynchoids are the oldest flying reptiles that ever existed. They were all small, with a long snout and fine, pointed teeth. Two wings of stretched skin between the fourth finger of their hand and the side of their body helped them fly. They had a long tail with a diamond-shaped end, which they used as a rudder to steer in the air.

SHORT-TAILED PTEROSAURS

First making an appearance during the Jurassic period, pterodactyloids gradually replaced their rhamphorhynchoid ancestors. Armed with a very short tail, some had a beak in place of teeth. A few, like **Quetzalcoatlus**, reached a record size of over 46 feet from one wingtip to the other—in other words, the size of a small airplane!

DINOSAURS AND BIRDS

Dinosaurs such as **Microraptor** had genuine feathers on their limbs, forming wings that let them glide from tree to tree. Others, like *Confuciusornis*, became real birds and could fly by flapping their wings. They all still had jaws full of teeth, so it was best to keep out of biting distance!

VOLATICOTHERIUM THE FLYING MAMMAL

Despite its hairy body and the flaps of skin connecting its front and back paws, **Volaticotherium** was not a peaceful flying squirrel. This very distant cousin used its gliding wings to hunt insects, which it ate by piercing their shells with its small pointy teeth.

BAT-DINO

As big as a pigeon, the theropod **Yi qi** featured a strange long bony rod at its wrists. The rod supported a wing made of stretched skin, like a bat's. These unusual wings only let it glide from branch to branch—enough to hunt or evade predators.

XIANGLONG!

Much like the modern *Draco volans*, which is found today in Southeast Asia, **Xianglong** was a small lizard with wings on the sides of its body that helped it glide long distances. Flying and gliding are clearly the way to go when danger threatens!

IT'S A TRAP!

The world of the Mesozoic Era was littered with fatal traps. Suffocating gases, mud swamps, and violent sandstorms made dinosaurs and other animals their victims. Getting caught in a trap was bad luck for prehistoric creatures, but finding the location of a trap is good luck for today's paleontologists! Long-ago traps are now full of amazing fossils.

TRAPS FOR PREDATORS

For heavy animals like dinosaurs, swamps and other deep muddy areas could be fatal traps. Once they were bogged down in the mud, they could no longer move, and became easy prey for carnivores. Predators arrived in large numbers to feast on the ensnared animal. Bad move: The predators got stuck too, and starved because they couldn't hunt.

SANDSTORMS

In dry environments, windstorms suddenly moved mountains of sand. Many dinosaurs like *Oviraptor*, which incubated its eggs at the edge of the desert, got buried trying to protect their precious young . . . and ended up fossilized.

AN UNLIKELY HUG

80 million years ago an epic battle took place between a **Velociraptor** and a **Protoceratops**. While the two were tightly intertwined—the claws of the *Velociraptor* stuck in the body of its prey, and the teeth of the *Protoceratops* biting the foot of its attacker—a storm covered them with sand and stuck them in this position for all eternity!

THE POMPEII OF DINOSAURS

Living near a volcano can be dangerous. When the mountain erupts, clouds of burning, suffocating ash fill the area and kill all the creatures unlucky enough to be in the neighborhood. Many dinosaurs, such as **Microraptor**, paid the price and ended up at the bottoms of lakes with other volcano victims.

THE INVISIBLE KILLER

Near volcanoes, lethal, odorless natural gas can collect in sunken areas. Animals reckless enough to venture near these spots soon fainted, then died because they couldn't breathe. The smell of dead animals attracted predators who were often fooled in turn by this invisible trap!

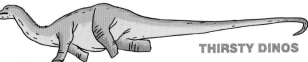

THIRSTY DINOS

The lack of water in deserts meant danger for dinosaurs. If a dinosaur ventured out too far, it risked dying of dehydration, or of the heat. It had to find shelter quickly to protect itself from the burning sun, and wait for the coolness of night. But if the sun didn't get a dinosaur, hunger and thirst might.

LIFE IN THE CRETACEOUS PERIOD
66 TO 145 MILLION YEARS AGO

In the Cretaceous, Earth's climate grew hotter. Flowering plants appeared at last and spread across the world. Tons of new dinosaurs arose to take advantage of the toasty planet. Sauropods saw their territories invaded by strange herbivores—iguanodons and marginocephalia—while stegosaurs gave way to ankylosaurs. There was also a revolution among predators, with the monstrous *Spinosaurus*, the colossal *Giganotosaurus*, and the treacherous *Velociraptor* leading a reign of terror over the other dinosaurs . . .

FIND THEM ALL!

SPINOSAURUS, THE SWIMMING DINOSAUR

How do you get ahead when your territory is full of other predators? **Spinosaurus** found a solution. Over time it became amphibious, spending part of its time on land and part swimming in waterways far from other theropods. Its favorite prey? The wealth of fish it caught with its long snout full of pointy teeth.

THE ORIGIN OF SNAKES

Snakes are descended from lizards whose bodies got longer and whose legs disappeared over the course of evolution. In the Cretaceous some of them, such as **Simoliophis**, still had their hind legs. Did losing their limbs allow the first snakes to swim faster by wiggling their bodies, or to move through tunnels underground? Paleontologists are still trying to answer this question.

IGUANODONS

Iguanodons, such as **Ouranosaurus**, and hadrosaurs are a group of quadruped or biped dinosaurs that lived all over the world. These herbivores possessed super-strong jaws with hundreds of teeth that helped them chew greens, grinding plants into tiny pieces. There were so many of them that paleontologists nicknamed them the "sheep of the Cretaceous."

SAUROPODS OF THE CRETACEOUS

The stars of the Jurassic, like *Diplodocus* or *Brachiosaurus*, gave way to new sauropods such as the strange **Nigersaurus**, whose skull looked like a vacuum cleaner head! Titanosaurs, another group, had backs covered in protective bony plates. At a length of over 116 feet, the titanosaur *Argentinosaurus* holds the record for biggest dinosaur!

GIANT THEROPODS

Some carnivorous dinosaurs were so huge that they could tackle great sauropods and iguanodons. One theropod, *Giganotosaurus*, grew over 46 feet long! Two groups of theropods with enormous heads but ridiculously small arms shared the planet. Tyrannosaurids ruled in the North and abelisaurids, like **Rugops**, in the South.

CROCODILES

Taking advantage of the Cretaceous heat, crocodiles multiplied and adapted to different lifestyles. Some of them had funny heads: **Kaprosuchus**, for example, looked like a warthog. Others became gigantic: *Sarcosuchus* reached a length of 40 feet. Still others had long legs that allowed them to gallop on land!

LIFE IN THE OCEANS

There were places where dinosaurs did not venture: the seas. In fact, no marine dinosaur has ever been discovered. On the other hand, numerous ocean reptiles, even larger and more terrifying, rode the waves. Ichthyosaurs, plesiosaurs, mosasaurs, turtles, and saltwater crocodiles fought over the prey of the seas: fish, crustaceans, ammonites, belemnites, and more. Luckily, all these predators did not exist at the same time!

ICHTHYOSAURS

They may look like dolphins, but don't be fooled. *Ichthyosaurs* were fierce reptiles with long snouts and mouths full of pointy teeth, perfect for stabbing prey. They breathed air and swam to the surface every so often for a breath. Unlike other reptiles, they did not lay eggs. Their young were born already swimming.

PLESIOSAURS

These enormous marine reptiles reached a length of 50 feet from the head to the tip of the tail. They had an unusually long neck, and oar-like limbs that helped them paddle through the water. Their preferred meals? Crustaceans, snails, and shellfish, which they grabbed from the ocean floor.

MOSASAURS

Making their appearance at the end of the Cretaceous, **mosasaurs** were giant reptiles similar to monitor lizards, with ocean-adapted bodies that made them unstoppable predators. Unlike ichthyosaurs and plesiosaurs, which swam the high seas, mosasaurs remained near the shore, where they ambushed their prey.

AMMONITES AND BELEMNITES

These animals—cousins of the octopus, squid, and nautilus—filled the oceans of the Mesozoic. Large marine reptiles hunted them as prey, but they were also predators, using their tentacles to seize an animal and devour it with their sharp mouths. The largest among them measured nearly six and a half feet across!

FISH AND SHARKS

Fish and sharks evolved long before marine reptiles, and remained very plentiful in the oceans. Some predatory fish, such as *Xiphactinus*, measured more than 20 feet long. And yet they were no match for the 40 feet of mosasaurs!

SALTWATER CROCODILES

The Mesozoic oceans were rich in prey, a bonanza for predators. Hungry crocodiles went to sea. **Thalattosuchians** ("ocean crocodiles") transformed through evolution to become fast, efficient swimmers on the open seas. Some of them even changed their tails into fins.

THE END OF A REIGN

66 million years ago, three quarters of all animals and plants disappeared from the Earth. Dinosaurs never recovered from this catastrophe, called the Cretaceous-Paleogene extinction, or the K-Pg extinction. But the land and sea did not remain empty for long. Other animals, like birds and mammals, used the end of the reign of reptiles to conquer the continents and become the new masters!

THE LAST DINOSAURS

Just before the extinction crisis began, many dinosaurs roamed the continents. In North America, for example, the predator **Tyrannosaurus rex**, the herbivore *Triceratops*, the duck-billed dinosaur *Parasaurolophus*, and the enormous *Alamosaurus* lived in the lush forests of the Cretaceous, full of conifers and flowering plants.

THE DECCAN TRAPS

Many animals died from the eruption of gigantic volcanoes in India, whose lava flows covered vast areas more than twice the size of Texas. These volcanic zones are called the "Deccan Traps." During the eruptions, large quantities of toxic gases and ash were dispersed into the sky, and may have disrupted the world's climate.

THE ASTEROID

At the end of the Cretaceous, colossal meteorites crashed into Earth, forming craters that measured miles across. The famous Chicxulub Crater in Mexico was hollowed out by an asteroid more than six miles wide—about half as long as Manhattan! Its massive impact doomed most of the plants and animals on earth.

AN ENDLESS NIGHT

Besides sparking off explosions, fires, and tsunamis, the asteroid impact launched huge amounts of ash into the sky. The ash blocked the sun for months, perhaps even years. Without sunlight, plants died. Only seeds and roots survived.

NOTHING LEFT TO EAT

Without plants to eat, herbivorous dinosaurs soon died. When they were gone, carnivorous dinosaurs had no food either, and starved as well. Famine ruled the land and sea, and many animals became extinct.

THE SURVIVORS

While dinosaurs, pterosaurs, and ancient crocodiles became extinct, other animals survived the crisis. Among these fortunate ones were mammals, birds (which are descendants of dinosaurs), and reptiles such as crocodiles, tortoises, lizards, and snakes. Why did they survive? The answer remains a mystery.

FIND THEM ALL!

SEARCHING IN THE EARTH

The dinosaurs of the Mesozoic are gone, but we can find their petrified remains—fossils—hidden in rocks all over the world. For paleontologists, finding fossils is a treasure hunt that often begins with a lucky person spotting a few pieces of bone, and ends with a big expedition!

DISCOVERING DEPOSITS

It's incredibly rare for someone to come across a fragment of dinosaur bone or tooth. Once paleontologists learn that one has been found in a new place, they begin the work of prospecting. That is, they search the area to figure out where they will dig for fossils.

PREPARING THE TERRAIN

The rock containing fossils is often covered in plants, soil, and other rocks. These things need to be removed. Aided by workers, paleontologists begin digging with shovels and pickaxes. Sometimes they even use a mechanical shovel to clear the surface, which will then be carefully excavated.

THE EXCAVATION

Now the excavation itself begins, and construction tools are replaced by hammers, chisels, brushes, and knives. The rock is chipped away little by little until a fossil appears. The fossil is then very carefully removed, photographed, and numbered. The paleontologists note exactly where they found it.

PROTECTING THE FOSSIL

Fossils are extremely fragile. Before being sent to the laboratory for study, they are coated with a special paste that solidifies them, then covered in plaster, forming a large protective shell. Not until the fossil reaches the laboratory is the plaster removed. The fossil is then completely cleaned.

HOSTILE ENVIRONMENT

Dinosaur fossils are sometimes located in remote places with harsh climates, like hot deserts or the freezing Arctic. In these wild environments paleontologists often face dangerous animals, such as bears, snakes, or scorpions.

RETURN TO THE LABORATORY

The excavating mission comes to an end and the team prepares to bring the fossils back to the laboratory. Certain fossils, like sauropod bones, are so huge that the plaster can weigh several tons and must travel by truck. When the excavation area can't be reached by car, the researchers bring in a helicopter to take away the fossils and their equipment.

THE PALEONTOLOGISTS GET TO WORK

Back in the lab, the paleontologists are buzzing with excitement! First they have to take the fossils out of the crates, prepare them, protect them because they are so fragile, and study them. Scientists have high-tech equipment that allows them to analyze the smallest details of the fossils. The paleontologists' discoveries are presented at conferences and published in special journals so that everyone can learn about the new fossils.

FINAL PREPARATIONS

When the plaster shells protecting the fossils reach the lab, they are carefully opened, and the bones are removed from the rest of the rock with small hammers, needles, and chisels. Once completely free of the rock, the fossils are coated with a special paste. This protects them and makes them stronger.

STUDIED FROM EVERY ANGLE

In order to figure out what animal the fossil came from, paleontologists examine it, measure it with rulers and calipers, and compare it to already known fossils. If the fossil doesn't look like anything known, it belongs to a new species that needs to be named.

BACK-UP TECHNOLOGY

Sometimes the fossil is damaged and too fragile to touch. When this happens, paleontologists use scanners that photograph the outside and inside of the bones. The scientists then look at the photographs on their computers, and can study the fossil without ruining it.

EUREKA!

The fossil the scientists found belongs to a new dinosaur species. The discoverer writes a long report, with plenty of photos. She describes the fossil and suggests giving it a name in two parts. In 1905, for example, the bones of an unknown giant carnivorous dinosaur were discovered in North America. Scientists named it *Tyrannosaurus rex*.

THE HOUR OF GLORY

Each year large conferences bring together paleontologists from all over the world, as well as a few journalists. At these gatherings scientists present their discoveries in English, the official language of science. This is their opportunity to unveil the new dinosaur to the whole world.

THE COLLECTIONS GROWS

The study is finished. The fossilized bones are stored in a museum or in the laboratory's collection, where they will be preserved for as long as possible. Other paleontologists can borrow these fossils to compare them to future discoveries.

DINOMANIA

For more than a century, dinosaurs have fascinated people of all ages. Movies, books, games, museums, theme parks, and even food products fill dino fans with happiness. In some countries the discovery of the first dinosaur fossil is a national event; in others, the "terrible lizards" are depicted on coins and stamps. Maybe man's best friend isn't the dog but the dinosaur!

MUSEUM STARS

Every major natural history museum has a hall dedicated to dinosaurs. Visitors can admire a full-sized *Diplodocus*, count the many bones of *Allosaurus*, and discover the fascinating world of these fierce animals.

T-REX IN BOOKS

From the classic novel *Lost World* by Arthur Conan Doyle to the *Dinotopia* books by James Gurney, every library has books devoted to dinosaurs. Whether it's a book of facts, a chapter book, a picture book, or a magazine article, dinosaurs are everywhere.

AN OSCAR FOR VELOCIRAPTOR

Jurassic Park may be the most popular example of dinosaurs on the big screen, but there are many more dino movies. In 1914 the first dinosaur film, *Brute Force*, pitted prehistoric people against "terrible lizards." Over the years, dinosaurs got involved in many sci-fi trends, including robots in the film *Transformers 4*.

MOST POPULAR TOY

Dinosaurs have a place of honor in toy stores, whether as stuffed animals, figurines, costumes, or something else entirely. You can even play as a dinosaur, or a person among dinosaurs, in many video games.

FIREMAN? POLICEMAN? NO, PALEONTOLOGIST!

Dinosaurs don't only fascinate kids; plenty of dinomaniacs grow up to study dinosaurs as a job! If this sounds like something you want to do, you can start by learning about biology and geology. There are even whole university departments dedicated to dinosaurs!

GIANTS OF THE SMALL SCREEN

TV also broadcasts plenty of shows about dinosaurs, from documentaries like the excellent BBC *Walking with Dinosaurs*, to cartoons, to science fiction. With incredible new technology, animated dinosaurs seem almost real, and can make you forget that these animals went extinct well before humans existed.